G000254507

365 DAYS

★ ★ ★ ★ ★ ★ ★ ★ OF ★ ★ ★ ★ ★ ★ ★ ★

CALM

Yvette Jane

summersdale

365 DAYS OF CALM

Summersdale Publishers Ltd
46 West Street
Chichester
West Sussex
PO19 1RP
UK

www.summersdale.com

Printed and bound in the Czech Republic

ISBN: 978-1-84953-640-0

December 2015

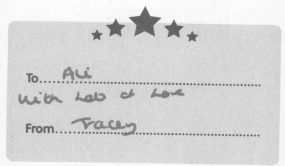

To...... Ali
With lots of Love

From...... Tracey

I hope you get lots of
enjoyment from this.

JANUARY

New Year's Day: Each new year brings fresh challenges and exciting opportunities. Endeavour to bring a sense of open curiosity to your experiences, rather than frustration when things don't go to plan.

 Introduce some de-stressing habits into your life – perhaps decide to switch off your mobile phone by a certain time each evening or make weekends television-free. Consider some other indoor activities you might do instead.

JANUARY

 Massage your scalp and the back of your neck with fingertip circular movements to ease the build-up of tension.

 Be sure to pause for a moment here and there throughout your day to stay composed and on top form. This might mean taking three mindful in-and-out breaths or a few relaxing stretches.

 Visit a local pub and cosy up in front of a blazing fire, and let it ease you into a warm sense of well-being.

 Carry hand cream in your bag and give your hands a nourishing mini-massage when you have a few moments to spare.

Focus on completing one task at a time – you're more likely to remain unflustered and make fewer mistakes. Remember, multitasking raises blood pressure.

 The new year is a great time for new projects. Before you start out, ask yourself what you wish to achieve. Imagine you have a clear space before you and set off unperturbed and completely focused.

 Tiny changes are easier to begin and to sustain than huge ones. Decide what small things you want to do to enhance your life, introduce them and keep on going!

10 If the weather is slightly sombre, find photos of fields of sunflowers, bluebells or poppies and breathe in the energy of their colours and the rays of sunlight.

11 Give yourself a minute to stop, close your eyes and visualise waves of calm flowing down through your body, from your head to your toes. Move on with a renewed sense of peace.

12 Keep your workplace, home and car clutter-free – you will feel a greater sense of stability and calm when your surroundings are tidy.

Quiet your mind. Breathe
and let go of words,
worry, and plans.

Doreen Virtue

Calmness of mind is one of the beautiful jewels of wisdom.

James Allen

JANUARY

 15 Regular meditation is a tried-and-trusted means of quieting the mind and gaining a sense of tranquillity. Seek a meditation class to learn this valuable skill.

 16 Spend an hour or so browsing in a local library, where you will be surrounded by knowledge, imagination and peace.

 17 If you are rushing about at home doing lots of chores, put on some soothing music to help you remain unruffled. Enjoy a sense of achievement when you are finished.

Be still and bring your awareness to your breath. Take some deep breaths, focusing on the movement of your abdomen as it rises and falls. This will slow your heart rate and soothe your mind.

 Light a candle and sit in stillness as you gaze into the flame. Allow its warm glow to illuminate you with radiance.

 Keep a great-smelling citrus or floral aromatherapy salve near by to dab onto your hands, lips, wrists and elbows. Breathe in and enjoy the tranquil aroma.

Be patient. Sometimes things feel chaotic, but stop and pause. Focus on taking two or three breaths, to calm you down and encourage your self-possession.

 Cook up a nourishing hotpot or casserole and share with family and friends. Laughter, good food and company are an antidote to stress.

 On your homeward journey, if you have a daily commute by train or bus, allow yourself 15 minutes to daydream and simply switch off. This provides a useful transition between work and arrival at home.

24 If you constantly find you start each morning rushing around like a dervish, set your alarm 15 minutes earlier and see how a calm start can make all the difference to your day.

 25 Stay warm and cosy during the winter evenings with an embroidery project or another craft activity you enjoy doing.

 26 If the winter months bring snow, enjoy a moment to stop and watch the magic of falling snowflakes. Capture the feeling of serenity and carry it with you through your day.

Be the calm center in the raging flow of life.

Leo Babauta

More haste, less speed.

Proverb

Allow a gentle smile to your lips and see how this encourages you to feel lighter and less troubled.

 As you prepare food in the kitchen, slow down and peel potatoes, chop carrots or wash broccoli with a mindful sense of purpose.

 Make up your own phrases that you find meaningful and helpful to recite:
Tranquillity lead the way.
Calm sit beside me.
Stillness surround me.
Compassion in my heart.

FEBRUARY

1 Talk less. Notice how it may lead to you doing things with a quieter, more mindful approach.

2 It can often be that those we love the most experience our short tempers and frayed nerves. Try counting several of your breaths before you turn the air blue and say words you may regret.

3 Get out your old photographs and reminisce about happy times gone by.

Be flexible – take your cue from nature, since grasses bend in the wind but sometimes trees are blown over.

 Recharge your batteries by attending a retreat – be it a health spa or centre for well-being. Anything from a weekend to a month could be just what you need.

 It might seem strange, but allowing yourself moments of repose actually reinvigorates you. Give it a go!

Keep your garden bird feeder topped up and watch the antics of winter visitors enjoying their much-needed snacks.

 Your body works best in 90-minute energy cycles. When you notice you are easily distracted from your task, take a ten-minute break to restore you to your peak performance.

 When you look into the mirror, allow your eyes to settle on your face. With a steady gaze, affirm to yourself, 'I am calm, I am peaceful.'

Set peace of mind as your highest goal, and organize your life around it.

Brian Tracy

Tension is who you think you should be. Relaxation is who you are.

Chinese proverb

Sometimes a busy mind can feel overwhelming. Keep a diary to express your thoughts and gratitude, and notice how focusing on the positive eases life's stresses.

 Go out and buy some fluffy new bath towels to make the simple things in life more comforting.

 If tension is building up, allow yourself a chance to stretch your body, flex your joints and loosen your muscles. If you have more time, go for a tranquil swim or a replenishing yoga class.

15 Curl up with a book that you've been meaning to read for some time or return to a treasured familiar story.

 16 Attach a note on the dashboard of your car, or the edge of your laptop, with a reminder: 'Stay centred', 'Breathe deeply' or 'I am peaceful'.

 17 If you travel to work by bus or car, use every red traffic light as an opportunity to ground yourself with a feeling of balance and centred calm.

18 You can't control everything so don't even try! Be relaxed yet alert whatever your task.

 19 If you're struggling with something, stop a moment to remember that you are doing the best you can. Your intentions are good, so remember to feel good too.

 20 Buy yourself a large jigsaw puzzle. Start it and keep it out somewhere handy for a satisfying winter evening activity.

 21 Live every day as though it were your first – with curiosity, openness and wonder.

22 Whether you are in the shower or the car, sing along to your favourite tunes. The benefits of singing include lower blood pressure and reduced stress.

 23 Tap into the part of you that feels soft and gentle towards other people – your compassion and kindness. Become aware of how often you feel compassionate or kind, and focus on how good it feels.

 24 When you perceive something as stressful your brain elicits a stress response; it prepares you for a fight or for flight. Gain perspective by focusing on your breath, which creates a sense of repose.

Quiet *is* the new loud.

Patrick Stump

Worry pretends to be necessary but serves no useful purpose.

Eckhart Tolle

27 Keep an aromatherapy room spray to hand, so that you can freshen the air with relaxing orange blossom or French lavender.

 28 Are you having a laugh? Combat stress with regular doses of your favourite cartoons and comedy programmes.

 29 Display a purple amethyst crystal in your home, as it is a good conductor of calm and peacefulness.

MARCH

1 Hugs from family and friends are great for raising levels of your feel-good hormone, oxytocin, which boosts self-esteem and reduces stress.

2 Add peace lilies, potted palm plants and vases of freshly cut flowers to your surroundings, creating a restful haven in which to work or relax.

3 Slow down! Wherever you walk, notice your surroundings and let your movements be measured and at ease.

Equanimity is neither apathy nor indifference: you are warmly engaged with the world but not troubled by it.

Rick Hanson

You can't calm the storm,
so stop trying. What you
can do is calm yourself.
The storm will pass.

Timber Hawkeye

MARCH

 Do something mad in March, perhaps flying a kite, learning kick-boxing or paintballing; a sense of exhilaration may be followed by a feeling of refreshment and a deep, rejuvenating sleep.

 Put together old-fashioned scrapbooks, filled with tickets and leaflets from places you have visited. This will make for a pleasant activity and create a joyful record to look back on in years to come.

 Experience a hot-stone massage and let the warmth absorb slowly and deeply into your skin.

9 When you are relaxed your brainwaves slow from beta activity to alpha activity; this enables you to deal with life with greater calm, clarity and objectivity. Make relaxing a small part of your day today.

 10 While away an afternoon in an art gallery, antique centre or bookshop.

 11 Identify your personal daily cycle – are you a morning, afternoon or evening person? Your awareness of this can help you manage your time more effectively.

MARCH

 Drinking caffeinated coffee can raise your blood pressure so limit your daily intake to no more than two cups or switch to cool, refreshing water.

 If stressful situations are getting you down, sit and share with a friend who you know will listen to you without judgement. Notice how your heart feels lighter afterwards.

 Set yourself the task of giving your home a spring clean. Not only will your surroundings gleam but any stress you were feeling will have been swept away in the process.

World Sleep Day: Find some tranquillity by enhancing the peacefulness of your bedroom. Invest in some blackout blinds, earplugs, a luxurious mattress or anything else that will make each night's sleep perfect.

Keep a sense of equilibrium and be adaptable to change at work by tapping in to the element of water, which is fluid and free-flowing.

Turn a regular evening meal into something special by filling the room with candlelight.

When you want to stay calm through a problem, visualise the most unflappable person you know. Emulate their demeanour, moving slowly, with purpose and a quiet voice.

 Be mindful for one minute every hour – sit still, attune yourself to your body and your breath.

Spring Equinox: Look forward to warmer weather with growing joy and contentment. As a sign of your optimism, decorate your home with some bright spring flowers.

21 Manage feelings of impatience by remembering to pause before you react. You can then make a clear choice in how you behave.

 22 Bring your complete focus onto the ironing, washing-up or dusting. Place all other worries to one side, and you may be amazed at how calming household chores can be!

 23 When you arrive home after a busy day's work, ease yourself into a more relaxed mode with an evening ritual. Take some deep breaths after entering, sip some water or wash your hands.

Contentment is natural wealth, luxury is artificial poverty.

Socrates

Let peace be your middle name.

Ntathu Allen

Soothe tired eyes by placing a slice of cucumber on each one for 10 minutes.

 Take a springtime walk in woodlands, a park or garden and use all your senses to experience the new life budding around you.

 Try eating meals that are low in glycaemic load, which means they are not full of sugar. Porridge, scrambled eggs on toast or vegetable soup will keep your energy levels steady and help you to maintain a level mood.

Buy yourself some worry beads, known in Greece as *kombolói*. Use the string of coloured beads as a beautiful calming distraction for your hands.

 Regular relaxation boosts your immune system and reduces high blood pressure. Join a class for something you thoroughly enjoy – perhaps cookery, photography or writing.

 Avoid negative thinking as much as possible – it drains you of energy. Look for the triumphs, however tiny they are!

APRIL

 1 Listen to the birdsong outside your window. Let those tiny creatures of optimism encourage you to sing your own songs of joy and goodwill.

 2 Set aside an afternoon to get creative decorating eggs. Have fun with colour and textures and enjoy the delight of your friends on receiving these as gifts.

 3 Set aside some time over the weekend when you don't have anything planned. See where it takes you.

Always look for the learning in a situation, especially when it doesn't turn out as anticipated.

 Monitor your posture as you go about your day. Adjust rounded shoulders or a stooping back. Consciously bring a sense of dignity to your presence.

 Rub a drop of lavender oil directly onto your temples or add to a warm bath. The oil's properties help reduce muscle tension and promote a sense of calm.

Nature teaches us simplicity and contentment, because in its presence we realize we need very little to be happy.

Mark Coleman

The best response to any difficult situation is to keep your calm.

Lailah Gifty Akita

If you are sitting exams or attending an interview, prepare yourself beforehand by breathing steadily. Remain calm and collected and you will give your best performance.

 Arrange a jug of spring flowers and quietly enjoy the whole process in an otherwise busy day.

 If you are living fast and furiously, you are missing all your moments. Each moment composes your life, so slow down and you won't miss a thing!

Exercise is a great way to break the cycle of anxiety. Meet up with friends and exercise together for motivation and more fun.

 Buy a notebook in which to record your thoughts, dreams and ideas. Enjoy quiet moments of thoughtful scribbling.

 Become a pet owner – animals can cheer you up and help you feel loved and relaxed.

15 Grow plants on a rooftop, patio or balcony if you don't own a garden. This reaffirms your connection to the cycle of life and develops patience, curiosity and joy.

 16 As you arrive at work, greet each person you see and resist the urge to rush on past.

 17 Go to the kitchen and bake away your stress. Unwind the tension as you measure and mix cake ingredients followed by the satisfaction of sharing a slice with friends or family.

Giggling with a friend is a much underrated pursuit. Spend time with someone who shares your sense of humour and remember – you can be 25 or 105 for this to work!

 Be more selective and say 'no' to requests when you already have a packed schedule.

 Getting constantly distracted is a recipe for frustration and stress. Daily meditation strengthens your ability to focus on one thing at a time. You are then more productive in your work because you resist distractions.

Better to do a little well than a great deal badly.

Socrates

Try to be like the turtle – at ease in your own shell.

Bill Copeland

23 Sometimes the best thing to do is relax your attitude and simply say, 'All will be well.'

 24 When you're relaxed, your brain is more receptive to creative and intuitive ideas. Try taking a few in-and-out breaths before tackling a challenge today.

 25 Spend the day at a nature reserve where you can hire a pair of binoculars and view birds and other wildlife close up.

26 Visualise, behind closed eyes, a peaceful place that you love. Calmly breathe while imagining you are there.

 27 Turn your bathroom into an oasis of calm with a new shelf to display your toiletries, fresh flannels and glass jars filled with soaps and other cleansing items.

 28 If you are speaking to an audience, it's worth remembering to be comfortable with pauses, use humour and work on your body language. You'll appear calm and confident!

Cultivate peace. Commit to peace. Insist on it.

Melody Beattie

There is a time to be quiet and a time to talk.

Aung San Suu Kyi

MAY

May Day: In the northern hemisphere today is a celebration of spring. If you're lucky enough to have the day off work, give the time over to pure relaxation.

 Picture the soft pink and white blossom of the hawthorn in a warm breeze and allow the image to soothe you. If you're able, take a walk out to the country and study this beautiful flower, which flourishes at this time of year.

If you are experiencing a travel delay, use this time to top-up your levels of tranquillity. Focus on yourself and breathe slowly until the standstill disperses and you are on your way.

 Consider starting a diary, as writing can be a great way to clarify thoughts and problem-solve.

 Treat yourself to a pedicure and glide smoothly on feather-light feet!

Keep this sentiment in mind today: define what is necessary for you to do and say 'no' to the rest.

 Notice if you have a frowning brow, a tense jaw or a grimacing mouth. Hold your warm hands across your face for a few seconds and let the tension subside.

How can you combine fun, increased good health and a reduction in your stress levels? Commit to a regular exercise class that you enjoy!

 Don't let the little annoying things in life get you down. Look at the bigger picture and get things into perspective.

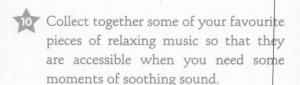

10 Collect together some of your favourite pieces of relaxing music so that they are accessible when you need some moments of soothing sound.

11 It's easy to give yourself a hard time with negative self-talk. Remember to give yourself a pat on the back now and then.

12 Wear bangles on your wrist or keep keys in your pocket. Allow the sound they make with your movements to be a reminder of awareness for the present moment.

 13 Optimise your sense of well-being by cutting back on sugary snacks – these induce a sugar high, followed by a dip in mood. Use your eating habits to help you achieve a more regulated sense of calm.

Watch the fish in a tank, aquarium or pond for 30 minutes and your blood pressure will become significantly lower.

 Take small actions to encourage greater focus. Set aside blocks of time to deal with emails, update social media pages and make phone calls, instead of haphazardly dipping in and out.

Before you leave your bedroom each morning, look out of the window at the sky and feel connected to the wonder of nature.

 Being calm doesn't mean you never take risks. Today, consider if you would like to make any changes in your life and be grounded and peaceful, whatever you decide to do.

Cats are portable calm distributors. They're like vending machines distributing peace for free.

Jarod Kintz

Equanimity is a perfect, unshakable balance of mind.

Nyanaponika Thera

20 If you love what you are doing, you will be content and happy. If you don't, look for ways to change this.

 21 There is always something to see on your travels. Ease up and appreciate what is around you.

 22 As you sit to eat breakfast, enjoy a calm oasis without distractions from the television, gadgets or smartphones as you prepare for your day.

In your free time, choose outdoor activities that fully engross you. Horse riding, sailing or archery are challenging yet enjoyable, and offer relief from stressful thoughts.

 Drink a herbal tea with relaxing properties, such as camomile, lime flower or lemon balm.

 Write a postcard to send to a friend or family member. Enjoy the process of looking for the perfect card and writing a few loving words.

A man of calm is like a shady tree. People who need shelter come to it.

Toba Beta

So the pie isn't perfect?
Cut it into wedges. Stay in
control, and never panic.

Martha Stewart

Get moving! Regular aerobic exercise reduces worry and increases the body's natural endorphins such as serotonin and dopamine.

 Keep an eye out for local events like May fairs and farmers' markets. Enjoy having a potter around your local community and chatting with the people you meet.

 Remember to be thankful for everything you have.

 Get plenty of sleep, since this is a precious component of your good health.

JUNE

 Take a trip on a canal barge or rowing boat on a local lake. As you glide across the ripples of the water, let yourself feel a sense of flowing relaxation.

 Build your confidence levels by creating your own positive statement. Repeat this to yourself as you go to sleep each night. This will reduce feelings of self-doubt and help your self-belief.

 Stay positive to stay calm.

Radiate peace. Who knows? The peace you spread may create the only restful place in your environment.

Stella Payton

Without accepting the fact that everything changes, we cannot find perfect composure.

Shinichi Suzuki

Expect a planned event to go without a hitch — set your intention to be calm and collected, and able to magnificently manage everything that happens today.

 Sometimes our thoughts are self-critical and negative. In this instance, focus on your breath and allow its subtle movements to gently guide you back to positivity.

 Keep a book of inspirational quotes by your bedside so that you can dip into it when at peace, at night or in the morning.

Before you begin something today, pause and ask yourself why you are doing it. Be clear about your intentions then focus fully on what you must do.

 Let your meandering mind slow down with a short session of meditation. This allows you to reduce the feeling of being overwhelmed, and take a more considered approach.

 Choose the traits of a favourite wild animal – the courage of a lion or the freedom of an eagle. Visualise what is suitable for you and embody what you most need right now.

Iron deficiency in your diet can make you feel tired and grumpy. Eat plenty of fresh vegetables, grains and pulses to keep on top of this.

 As you hang washing out on the line, notice the sound of the birds, smell the clean clothes and fresh grass, and turn a household chore into a simple pleasure.

 If you have experienced something especially stressful today, make sure you restore your balance as soon as possible by meditating, sharing with trusted friends or getting some exercise.

Flowers have a language of their own. For serenity choose lavender, for peace choose hazel or olive branches and for simplicity choose a wild rose.

 When you are relaxed your brainwaves slow down and allow you to access the creative part of your brain. Take this chance to find inspiring solutions in place of automatic answers.

 Stop trying to change others! Enjoy the time you spend with loved ones without the need to give them advice. Accept the annoyances of colleagues and focus on the positives.

Take rest; a field that has rested gives a bountiful crop.

Ovid

Your mind will answer
most questions if you learn
to relax and wait for the
answer.

William S. Burroughs

20 Go for a bike ride away from traffic and enjoy the sense of freedom you feel as you roll gently through a quiet lane.

 21 Wake up in time to welcome the sunrise – a daily feat of nature that you may often miss. Let its calm grandeur vibrate through your body for the rest of the day.

 22 Download a meditation or relaxation app and listen to it regularly as a means of managing stress and experiencing tranquillity.

23 When you feel under pressure, resist the urge to dramatise your experience either to yourself or to others. Reframe it as a challenge that you can rise to with confidence.

 24 Check you have the best working conditions to suit you. Ask yourself: is it too hot or cold? Getting overheated on a summer's day can overstress the body and slow you down.

 25 Choose your favourite music for singing or dancing along to. It's a quick and fun solution to lower those levels of stress and inject some cheerfulness into your day!

If you are cycling or walking, notice how different it is when you are not listening to music on your headphones. Have a change and experience less din.

 Get swept off your feet and experience the exhilaration and quiet calm of a hot-air balloon ride.

If you have challenges to meet today, think about them on a scale of one to ten, with the highest as the most challenging. Most people find their challenges fall between two and five. This puts it all into perspective.

 Schedule in rewards! It's great to have things to look forward to and enjoy after all your efforts.

 Keep family photos on your desk at work. They can be a lovely reminder of happiness in your life.

JULY

National Motivation Day (UK): Shift your perspective and tell yourself that you 'choose' to do things rather than you 'have' to do them.

If you feel like you're losing focus or being swept away in a busy rush, count backwards from 100 to zero, so that you centre and turn your attention back to the task at hand.

Take every opportunity to enjoy the balmy days of summer and replenish your levels of vitamin D.

 Plan a picnic by the shores of a lake and allow the placid view to calm your senses.

 Visit an arboretum or woodland and let the hushed secrecy of the trees fill you with cool composure.

Make a refreshing jug of flavoured water and leave it to chill overnight in the fridge. Experiment with your favourite flavours: try lemon and cucumber slices with a sprig of mint, or sliced ginger and pineapple.

 Develop a flexible mind and everything becomes easier, as you are open to changes around you. Start by accepting yourself, flaws and all!

 Use your local park or green space to play Frisbee or rounders with friends. Relax and have fun!

9 Enjoy an untroubled afternoon tea with a friend. Savour each mouthful and relish every moment of friendship.

 10 If it is possible, walk or cycle part, or all, of the way to work. This regular exercise can set you up for the day.

 11 Find a quiet spot next to running water, perhaps a bubbling brook or a little water fountain. Allow the sound to soothe your troubled mind.

If you act anxiously to hasten your results, you delay their arrival. Calm poise reveals the shortest route home.

Alan Cohen

Stop a moment,
cease your work,
look around you.

Leo Tolstoy

Enjoy a sporting activity where body and mind work together to encourage a feeling of buoyancy and fun. Try water skiing, rowing or wild swimming.

 Lie outside on the grass and gaze up at the sky above you.

 Remember you have five senses with which to experience life – sight, sound, touch, smell and taste. Pace yourself so you overlook nothing.

17 Treasure halcyon days spent with family and friends. As you experience joyful memories your health also benefits from spending time with those you love.

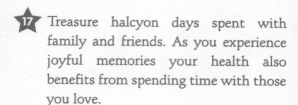

18 Stay calm and composed by wearing natural, lightweight fabrics.

19 A great tip to help stay calm and unflappable is to go to the bathroom and wash your hands and wrists slowly under cooling water.

I will be calm. I will be mistress of myself.

Jane Austen

Remain calm, serene,
always in command
of yourself. You will
then find out how easy
it is to get along.

Paramahansa Yogananda

22 Grab your bucket and spade and spend a few leisurely hours rock pooling at the coast. Marvel at the hushed 'other worlds' you may find.

 23 Share news of your successes today. It encourages and inspires others while building up your sense of well-being!

 24 Chill out in a hammock or comfy chair in the back garden and make the most of sunny days.

 25 Visit a rose garden and spend an hour of delight absorbing the diverse colours and perfumes.

If you find the sound of flowing water to be soothing, invest in a mini-fountain for your garden or outdoor area.

 Stop stressing about the negative things and appreciate all your blessings.

 Find creative answers to problems by sleeping on them – the transitional moments when you first awake from sleep can often throw up unexpected answers.

Disconnect to a sanctuary of calm. It might be ten minutes sitting quietly in your car or an hour out of sight in a corner of your garden. Respect your need for 'alone time'.

 If you are travelling on holiday by plane or train, allow plenty of time so you are not likely to arrive late – a relaxing holiday starts with a stress-free connection!

 Escape into nature with your ears! Download and listen to crashing waves, whale song or a rainforest soundscape.

AUGUST

 When you are on holiday, or being a tourist for the weekend, don't 'schedule' too many things. Enjoy simply being in another place.

 Walk barefoot on grass or sand to give your feet a massage and feel connected to nature.

 Take a trip to the seaside and let the sparkling waves mesmerise you with their unhurried rhythm.

AUGUST

 Particularly on hot nights, use a feather or down pillow with a cotton pillowcase, as synthetic pillows retain heat. Enjoy a cool and tranquil sleep.

 Lower your chin and notice how often you might be holding your head out of alignment with your neck and spine. This awareness reduces the build-up of tension through the day.

World Meditation Day: Find a meditation workshop event near you and give it a try.

Sit beneath a tree. Enjoy its dappled shade and the gentle sound of wind swaying the branches.

 Address the issues of good nutrition and hydration, some exercise and plentiful sleep. These are the fundamental basics that can help you cope with stressful times.

 Enjoy the chance to sit outside and watch the sun setting. Bathe in the colours and absorb the warm rays as they slide towards the horizon.

Never hurry and never worry!

E. B. White

It is neither wealth nor splendor; but tranquillity and occupation which give you happiness.

Thomas Jefferson

AUGUST

 Don't lose your inner composure by comparing yourself to anyone else. Maintain your own set of values and follow these.

 Regular running or steady walks are beneficial in many ways and are great mood-improvers. Get those sports shoes on!

 Feel refreshed and glowing by using a delicate face spray.

 Surrender! It doesn't mean giving up — it is acceptance, which then empowers you to move on.

When your body is under stress it is working harder and this drains your immune system. Slow down and endeavour to stay calm – it gives you the edge on good health.

 What circumstances press your stress buttons the most? Become aware of your patterns of behaviour so that you know which strategies are effective for you.

 Be careful what you blog or tweet when experiencing problems. The advice or response of others may leave you feeling undermined or overwhelmed.

To sit in the shade on a fine day, and look upon verdure is the most perfect refreshment.

Jane Austen

Acquire inner peace and a multitude will find their salvation near you.

Catherine Doherty

AUGUST

 21 If you are struggling with a moment of panic, stop and observe your breathing. It may have become shallow, so inhale deeply and follow the rise and fall of your stomach.

 22 Sit out on a sunny day and sip a non-alcoholic cocktail of your choice with plenty of ice and a slice of lime.

 23 Get splashing! Plan a swim outdoors in the sea, a lake or a lido.

 24 If you are running, or doing other strenuous activity, on very hot days aim to do this in the cooler mornings before 7.00 a.m.

AUGUST

 25 Get together with work colleagues or family and friends for a BBQ and enjoy good food and good company.

 26 Don't skip meals or you will feel irritable and jittery – food is not just about nourishment, but also balances your mood.

 27 Make some bubble mixture with washing-up liquid and blow bubbles in the garden. Sometimes it's fun to do kids' stuff!

 28 Where the mind goes, the body follows so steer your thoughts to a calm presence and notice the tension drop away.

29 It's important to remember what it feels like to be calm and stress-free. Sometimes it feels more normal to be on an adrenaline rush, so step back and identify what you are experiencing.

 30 As you walk along the pavement bring awareness to your feet as you lift and place them on the ground. Be thankful for your feet as they carry you across the miles.

 31 Burn some calming aromatherapy oil, such as basil or rose, while you practise relaxation exercises or meditate. The scent enhances your sense of well-being and clarity.

SEPTEMBER

 Sign up for a class in qigong, t'ai chi or yoga and experience the pure calm of mindful movement.

 If you are feeling overwhelmed in a stressful situation, see if it's possible to take a short walk and return with a renewed perspective.

 In chaotic moments, place your hand over your heart and concentrate on steadying your heartbeat.

Nothing baffles the schemes of evil people so much as the calm composure of great souls.

Honoré Gabriel Riqueti, comte de Mirabeau

A hasty man drinks his tea with a fork.

Chinese proverb

Invest in a little self-massage roller, so you can ease tense muscles for a quick relaxation fix.

 Sink your weary body into a relaxing hot bath of herbs or aromatherapy oil. Soak away all your cares while your aching bones and joints soften and release their tension.

 Focus on your strengths and feel good about them. Nobody is an expert in everything, so enjoy the things at which you excel.

Walking meetings are a great way to burn off stress and get some fresh air, while still getting things done. If you've never tried one, suggest it today!

 When was the last time you did something you love doing? If it's been too long to remember, get planning and pick up the fun you left off.

 Stop and look out of your window at nature's changing seasons. Notice the cycles of nature and absorb their sense of harmony.

Mindfulness Day: Close your eyes and breathe as slowly as possible. Become aware of all the things you can feel: the weight of your body on your chair, your hair against your forehead, a slight breeze through a window.

Remember that you can choose your response in any situation. Know when to let go or when something needs to be addressed head-on.

Slow your pace as you eat. Appreciate and enjoy your food.

It's essential to regularly stop and ask yourself, 'How am I feeling?' With this awareness of what may be exhaustion, grumpiness or anger, you can ease back on careless overreactions.

 If you face a problem today, visualise it as a knot in a piece of rope. If you panic, the knot will tighten, but if you relax you experience a sense of loosening and relief.

 Take ten minutes in your day to lie down in a position recommended by the Alexander technique, with your spine relaxed along the floor, holding your knees bent and keeping your feet flat.

The beat of my heart
has grown deeper,
more active, and yet
more peaceful.

Etty Hillesum

Unhappy are they who lose their cool and are too proud to say, 'I'm sorry.'

Robert H. Schuller

Create a harmonious, relaxing environment in your bedroom by choosing calming colours for the walls. Choose from shades of white, pale blue or soft green.

 A peaceful mind creates a peaceful world.

Autumn Equinox: Let yourself bathe in the beams of luminous moonlight.

 Have you always wanted to learn the saxophone, guitar or drums? It's never too late and is a wonderful way to have fun, relieve stress and be creative.

Hold your eyes closed and relax them for a moment. Open them then repeat three times.

 If you need some peace and quiet, earplugs are a great way of blocking out unwanted distractions. You could also try putting on your headphones and playing some soothing music.

 At the weekend, a natural sunrise alarm clock produces slowly increasing light to awaken you. Combined with a gentle sound, it's the perfect way to start the morning as you mean to carry on.

27 Get mending jobs done promptly so they don't become annoying, such as replacing a broken lamp or putting up a bookshelf.

 28 Melatonin is the hormone that influences your sleep–wake patterns and requires plenty of daylight exposure. Get outside as much as you can!

 29 Book yourself a replenishing Japanese face massage. It involves gentle working of the acupressure points on the face and head.

 30 Take the chance to pick local apples and pears, enjoying the connection you feel with nature.

OCTOBER

1 Recover from a stressful event by sipping traditional black tea. Studies have shown that it reduces levels of the stress hormone cortisol.

2 Resist the temptation to book yourself back to back with appointments and tasks. Allow space for doing nothing in your timetable.

3 Release feelings of apprehension by affirming to yourself, 'I am strong. I can do this!'

Don't let a mad world
tell you that success
is anything other
than a successful
present moment.

Eckhart Tolle

Instead of wondering when your next vacation is, maybe you should set up a life you don't need to escape from.

Seth Godin

Listening to rumours and sharing gossip can sometimes spread stress like wildfire! See how it feels to avoid this for a week and you may be surprised how peaceful you feel.

 If you are decision-making, allow yourself time to write down all your options, drawing up a list of positives and negatives. That way, you are not making hasty, rushed choices.

 Listen to the wind rustling through the autumn leaves. Imagine it is sweeping away the cobwebs in your mind to make way for clarity.

Book yourself an aromatherapy massage and surrender to the gentle sense of touch and aroma. Leave with soft, supple skin and light footsteps as if walking on clouds.

 Be happy with less – if you are forever searching for the next item of clothing, the next car, the next house then your pursuit and your stress will never end.

 Accept what cannot be changed. Refusal creates inner turmoil and leads to a dead end.

Give yourself time to step outside and appreciate the golden colours of the autumnal leaves.

 Place a warm heat wrap around your neck and shoulders for 10 minutes. Close your eyes and relax the muscles of your face, neck, upper chest and back. Allow tension to dissolve.

 If you are a cat or dog owner you will know the great sense of well-being you experience when you cuddle and fuss your pet – if you're not, why not pay a visit to someone who is?

OCTOBER

 15 Relax and enjoy some seasonal baking – try poached plums, baked pears or apple and blackberry crumble.

 16 Visualise yourself walking downwards across sand dunes or fluffy clouds. With every step you feel more relaxed and comfortable until you stop. Sit for a few moments experiencing a deep sense of calm.

 17 Keep this sentiment in mind today: everyday, mundane events contain beauty and unexpected wonder when you look more closely.

Meditation is like a gym in which you develop the powerful mental muscles of calm and insight.

Ajahn Brahm

The key to everything
is patience. You get the
chicken by hatching the
egg, not by smashing it.

Arnold H. Glasow

Listen to yourself! Your body tells you when it needs a break, is hungry or wants sleep. Pay attention and take good care.

 Make your sofa and easy chairs welcome places to sink into with a selection of cushions that add colour as well as comfort to your home.

 Valerian root is a natural herb with relaxing effects. It promotes a feeling of soothing and calm, thus aiding sleep at night.

If you are feeling anxious, stand up straight with your feet placed in a wide stance. Like the roots of a tree, you have the earth's support. You are stronger than you think.

 Get creative with some Zen doodling. Drawing repetitive designs encourages a sense of calm and enormous satisfaction.

 Focus on your next action. If you look too far ahead, you might simply feel overwhelmed.

26 Use a pedometer to measure how many steps you take each day. This can be a great motivator to keep on the move and boost your serotonin levels.

 27 Never be afraid to ask for assistance either at home or work. When you are supported and well-organised, there's less need to panic and worry.

 28 Plant some pots of indoor-flowering bulbs so that when they emerge next spring you can display them on a windowsill or near your computer. Their scent and vivid colours will brighten your mood.

Switch off your work connections when you get home – checking emails and voicemails every evening and weekend means never taking time off. Your health will suffer.

 Organise some team-building activities at work. Everyone benefits from a reminder to share the load.

 Focus on your breathing. Keep your mouth closed and gently hum on each out-breath. This 'bee breathing' encourages you to slow down and deepen your breath, eliciting a calm response from your brain.

1 Become aware of your shoulders and allow them to relax down, away from your ears! As you do this, you open up the chest area and loosen tension across your whole upper body.

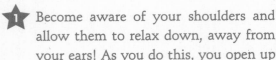 **2** Visualise a place of calm, like a beach, woodland or mountain scene.

 3 Remember to look at the night sky and experience amazement as you gaze up at the starlight.

4 Prepare for a good night's sleep by giving yourself time to unwind. Allow space to notice how you are feeling and navigate towards sleep by focusing on slow, easy breaths.

 5 Sweep up leaves and build a bonfire. Let these outdoor tasks energise you while enjoying the sounds and smells of autumn.

 6 Don't get caught up in checking your emails all day long. This increases your blood pressure and elevates your heart rate while distracting you from the job in hand!

Remain calm in every situation because peace equals power.

Joyce Meyer

When we are unable to find tranquillity within ourselves, it is useless to seek it elsewhere.

François de La Rochefoucauld

9 Enjoy the feel of soft hand-knitted scarves and jumpers against your skin, as you wrap up cosily through this chilly month.

 10 The best way to stay calm is to spot your stress levels before they rise too high. Choose your favourite tips in this book and use them as quick stress-busters.

 11 Stay composed and grounded by bringing your awareness to your feet. Notice your heels, toes and the balls of your feet inside your shoes and your connection to the earth.

When you are safely tucked up in bed and it's raining outside, allow the sound on the rooftops and windows to lull you to sleep.

 Perhaps you have noticed that you are more short-tempered, angry, irritable or overly anxious these days. These could be signs that you need to ease up and attend to your health and lifestyle.

 When you experience something happy, notice how easy it is to move on quickly, without appreciation. Stop and give your whole body time to soak up the feelings you are enjoying.

A free mind is one which is untroubled and unfettered by anything.

Meister Eckhart

Minds that are ill at ease are agitated by both hope and fear.

Ovid

17 Have an early afternoon nap to improve your mood and sense of well-being.

 18 Planning ahead can prevent potentially stressful situations from happening. Have a backup plan too, so that problems can be dealt with seamlessly.

 19 Plan your Christmas shopping for gifts now, so that during the festive season you won't be caught up in the chaos and are able to enjoy the fun.

Unchecked anger is a reaction that stems from the primitive, emotional part of your brain, as opposed to your rational, intellectual brain. Release negative emotions by seeking help and support.

 Even if you can't get out into nature, allow yourself to daydream while looking at pictures of mountains, the sea and forests.

 Lie back and listen to a recording of a novel or some recited poetry. Be transported to another world as you get swept along.

Sometimes your mind takes you along well-worn thought patterns. Ask yourself if you are predicting the worst outcome and judging yourself harshly. Stand back and let go of these constricting thoughts.

 Think about the lighting in your house and see how extra lamps or a dimmer switch could help you create areas of calm in which to relax.

 Get out your paintbrushes or drawing pencils and create canvasses expressing your feelings in colour.

26 Sometimes stress builds up because feelings haven't been expressed. Make time to speak with a trusted friend and share what is happening with you.

 27 It's so easy to get swept along in the serious business of work. Don't forget to smile as often as you can!

 28 Your body works in cycles of energy from higher to lower alertness. Take ten-minute breaks for exercise, a cuppa or a breath of fresh air. Return to your tasks in top form.

If you are feeling a little low or anxious, reflect on five things you can be thankful for. This is a great way to direct your mind towards gratitude when you have momentarily forgotten.

 Give yourself a quick massage: Relieve tense neck muscles by gently turning your head from side to side. Roll your shoulders up to your ears and down. Massage the back of your neck with your fingertips.

DECEMBER

 In the lead-up to Christmas, don't get overwhelmed with all that has to be done. Make a 'to-do' list and pace yourself by completing it one day at a time.

 Look into progressive muscle relaxation (PMR), which is a quick exercise in tensing then releasing the body's muscle groups. It involves an easy-to-learn format and allows you to feel less stressed within moments.

 Value the importance of enough sleep.

Walk as if you were kissing the earth with your feet.

Thích Nhất Hạnh

When something feels heavy, break it down until one piece of it is light enough to handle. Begin there.

Bernie S. Siegel

DECEMBER

 Stressful multitasking can feel disorientating and dissatisfying. Approach whatever you are doing in a methodical manner and enjoy an increased sense of achievement.

 Keep a colourful, soft blanket handy so that you can wrap up on chilly evenings, and feel safe and cherished.

 Stress balls are palm-sized balls made from foam or rubber. A few quick squeezes improves circulation and creates a sense of calm. They might even make great stocking fillers!

9 Enjoy a seasonal concert and soak up the sounds and sights of this festive time of year.

 10 Make a warm milky drink to enjoy on a chilly winter's night. Experiment by adding spicy cinnamon and ginger.

 11 Imagine that your turbulent thoughts are like clouds and they will pass. Welcome productive ideas and allow the negative ones to flow on by.

Keep your heart open and be strong.

Robert Holden

When lost in confusion, refer to present physical reality.

Chögyam Trungpa

As the end of the year draws near, the party mood kicks in. Try to maintain a sense of equilibrium by balancing your social outings with time for relaxation.

 Alcohol is a relaxant and may seem to be a great way to unwind in the evenings, but it also impairs the quality of your deep sleep, so consider a delicious soft drink instead.

 A light therapy box simulates sunshine and a daily dose can help keep your mood balanced when short winter days limit your exposure to sunlight.

Bring the beauty of nature into your house with a fir tree, fresh floral garlands and holly leaves full with clusters of berries. Let your senses be filled with texture, aroma and colour.

 Remember that others may have certain expectations at this time of year. Be clear about what is important to you, and focus on this.

 Use an aromatherapy burner to suffuse a sense of calm and tradition into the air with bergamot, cinnamon and sandalwood.

20 Don't get caught up in seasonal preparations that drain you of enjoyment. Share the tasks that need to be done and keep plenty of undisturbed evenings free to simply chill!

 21 If you have spent most of your year overwhelmed with stressful feelings, find out about hypnotherapy, which works on the deeper levels of your brainwaves. Perhaps you are ready for a positive change.

 22 Even if it's cold outside, wrap up warm, have a brisk walk and fill your lungs with some invigorating fresh air.

DECEMBER

 When you have expectations and life does not match them, you may feel dissatisfied. Instead, accept what is happening and go with the flow!

 Bring yourself back to a place of equilibrium by following the natural rhythm of your breath. It is with you wherever you go!

Christmas Day: Stop! Be present for each moment, as some of these may become precious memories.

26

Boxing Day: Have plenty of fun and games interspersed with a snooze on the sofa.

27 Nature retreats beneath the cold earth during winter and, for humans too, it is a time of hibernation. Replenish your energy with plenty of relaxation at home and with family.

28 Feel a calm sense of satisfaction as you spend time on a creative project such as knitting, sewing or painting.

DECEMBER

 Let your feet feel pampered in soft slippers.

 Relish and enjoy being with friends at this time of year. Having fun with those you love is a great way to relax and have plenty of laughs.

 Reflect on the positive moments of the year and consider how you can move forward into the next with calm and equilibrium.

If you're interested in finding out more about our books, find us on Facebook at **Summersdale Publishers** and follow us on Twitter at **@Summersdale**.

www.summersdale.com